# Irish Roses

## A Collection of Short Stories

Tall Tales by
Dorothy Mahon

# Irish Roses
*A Collection of Short Stories*

ISBN: 978-0-578-17710-6
ISBN: 978-0-578-17711-3 (e-book)

Cover design by Amy Cartee-Cox
Book design by Allan C. Kimball

 *Irish Roses* has been written in memory of Michael Mahon

**Blue Sky Communications**
homeonrange40@gmail.com
832-725-0440

# Contents

# Introduction

The stories in Irish Roses are original and based and embellished on the experiences I shared with my late husband, Michael, who was born in Dublin and resided in Brooklyn for many years of his life. The stories begin with an immigrant Irish woman named Rose crossing the ocean to America with her two young sons to start a new life in Brooklyn and progress to modern day young Irish American Roses, embracing or not embracing their Irish culture.

The idea of eventually tweaking and publishing Irish Roses came about several years ago while I was serving as an executive director of a Houston nonprofit.

We were seeking to develop a special event for fundraising and because Houston has countless events, the task was a difficult one. Since the nonprofit was newly formed, we wanted to tell our story but also entertain the audience.

The only dates not having an event were around Saint Patrick's Day, so we went forward with a luncheon fundraiser called *A Bit of the Blarney* featuring a storyteller telling stories that I wrote. It was a bit hit and done every year over a period of seven years.

It was great fun writing *Irish Roses,* I hope you enjoy the stories.

— *Dorothy Mahon*

# About The Author

Dorothy Mahon currently resides in New York City after living in Houston for over 35 years.  In Houston, she was a staff member of the *Houston Post* and then served as executive director of several Houston nonprofit organizations. In 1997, she was the recipient of the Women on the Move award presented by Texas Executive Women. The award recognizes Houston's top female executives who excel in their profession as well as contribute to community and charitable organizations.

Dorothy was born and educated in New York. Her Irish stories are based on the experiences shared with her late husband, Michael, who was born in Dublin and resided in Brooklyn for many years of his life. She is an advocate of the art of storytelling.

Dorothy is the mother of two daughters, Kate Shannon and Maggie Brie, and the grandmother of  Vivienne and Genevieve.

# A Little Bit Of Heaven Called Brooklyn

Rose Mulligan was a God-fearing woman who settled in Brooklyn after leaving Dublin in the year 1925. Rose left Dublin after her husband Patrick developed a fatal attraction to the Army of the Irish Republic and never returned. Rose knew there would be a hundred thousand welcomes for Patrick in the heavens of peace, and went about her way.

She was left with their two wee boys, Patrick and Michael. All of her kin lived in Dublin and were barely making a living wage; that is, all except her Uncle Simon. Uncle Simon now lived in America, Brooklyn, to be sure. Rose's family delighted in reading Simon's letters about his good fortune in his new land. Rose wanted a better life for her boys and was determined to leave Ireland for that little bit of heaven called Brooklyn.

She saved her money for the trip by renting out a tiny room in her flat and cooking, washing and ironing for her tenant. She was a brave woman to make the journey to America with her lads. She was a brave woman to make her home in Brooklyn. Over her lifetime Rose had many an adventure in Brooklyn but this is the one everyone remembers.

Uncle Simon always had a bit of the green in his pocket. No one was quite sure how it got there. No one ever asked any questions. Simon didn't have a shop or cart. He didn't go to an office. It appeared he didn't have a trade, but he did meet every day with a group of iron workers, the butcher, the baker, the tailor, the undertaker and most of the tradesmen in his neighborhood. Simon drove a General Motors car and lived in a grand three-story brownstone; Rose and her two sons lived on the ground floor. Rose worked for Simon as his bookkeeper. Each day, the neighborhood lads would knock on Rose's front door and give her an envelope. She would record their name, remove the money and give them their receipt.

One day, Shaun O'Leary, an ironworker, was banging the daylights out of Rose's door and demanding to see Simon. Shaun's reputation was one of a bully from the time he left his mother's womb, and thought to have not a brain in his head, by his neighbor, Mrs. Murphy.

Now, of course, you wouldn't have a brain in your head if you fell 12 stories from a building, as Shaun did. Poor Rose told Shaun that Simon wasn't home and to please leave in peace before she called Sgt. Kevin O'Reilly. Sgt. O'Reilly was an Irish American who had never been to Ireland, didn't much like the Irish, and certainly hated Irish cooking. He used to say, "Anyone who could identify the vegetable of the day in an Irish pub should get a free pint of Guinness." Much to Sgt. O'Reilly's dismay, no one was getting a pint of anything. Prohibition was in full force and Brooklyn was as dry as a turf fire.

Ah, Sgt. O'Reilly was sweet on Rose and was pleased to be invited to her table when asked. He even went along with her strange little Irish blessing that she gave every day: "Let us bank a fire in honour of Holy Patrick. May our house not be burnt or our people murdered. And may the bright sun of tomorrow shine on us all, at home or abroad."

Sgt. O'Reilly guessed more people were

murdered in Brooklyn in a year than the whole of Ireland, so maybe the blessing wasn't a bad thing.

Sgt. O' Reilly thought Rose's table had the comfort of the commonplace but that Rose had the look of having been here, there and everywhere. He was sure it was the crossing of the ocean that gave her that worldly look. Sgt. O'Reilly was indeed in love and would give his life, if need be, to save his Irish princess.

Shaun O'Leary was becoming a bit of a pest and banging on Rose's door every day of the week asking for Simon. Simon told Rose to pay no mind to Shaun. He knew what the problem was and he would handle it in his own good time. Simon's own good time was not time enough for Rose. Late on a Monday afternoon, Shaun came to Rose's door with the furry of fire in his eyes. Rose opened the door, Shaun grabbed her by her apron strings with her screaming all the while, "Shaun, you're a bad egg, a bad bird."

Shaun replied, "Simon's a dead duck if we don't get our money back."

Rose was slight of frame, barely tipping the scales at 100 pounds after her morning tea. She was no match for a brute like Shaun.

Shaun carried Rose into a big, bright, shinny black Cadillac. She had never been in a motor-car such as this and for a moment she stopped screaming to take a peek at the glory of the car. Shaun put a bit of tape over her mouth and blindfolded her, but not before she got a good look at the driver of the car. She knew he was no Irishman—an I-talian to be sure and dressed in a suit fit to be buried in. Rose gave a broken cry and wondered of the troubles that lay ahead.

The car sped off and came to a stop in a quiet place, so quiet that you could hear a cat's breath. Shaun and the I-talian put Rose in the lift and up they all went to the very top of the building. Shaun made his living by hanging off high buildings while holding his riveting gun. There were stories told that Shaun liked to hang by his bare feet from the highest point. Rose had never been higher than Mount Joy prison in Ireland. She was in a state of frantic bewilderment and downright sheer terror. I'm sure it can be told that Rose didn't appreciate a first rate tour of New York City's latest sky-scraper. Shaun guided Rose to an edge of the building and tied her hands and feet to a steel post.

Rose stammered, "This is a foolish thing you're doing, Shaun O'Leary."

Shaun replied, "Have ya ever known me to be wise? The deed is done, Rose. Be brave like Michael Collins, and pray to God that your Uncle Simon remembers he's related to you."

"Why in God's name are ya doing this to me?"

"Your Uncle Simon is running the largest underground still in Brooklyn, well, almost the largest. Al over here runs the largest."

"I don't know what you're saying."

"Rose, your uncle is a bootlegger. He's supplying all the pubs with beer and whiskey, not to mention your whole neighborhood including Father O'Rourke at St. Michael's. The only trouble is, lately he's been taking the money and not leaving a drop."

"Dear God, this can't be true. Shaun, you must be under the influence, you know, when the drop is inside the sense is outside."

"No, no, Rose, the three of us are on the outside, the 21st floor to be exact, and one of us is going down quicker than a fox running from a hound. If Simon doesn't come with the money he took from everyone by the stroke of eight, there'll be another Martyr for Old

Ireland."

Rose began to pray as she had never prayed before. "Dear God, you saw fit to save Ireland, please save me. I've done a foolish thing by coming to this place called Brooklyn. I only wanted the best for me Paddy and Michael. Please, God, don't wait 700 years before you answer me prayer."

Shaun left Rose alone with the I-talian gentlemen while he waited at the street level for Simon to come with the money. Rose starred straight ahead at the stars, not shedding a tear, and looking like the fine Irish lassie she was.

The I-talian man spoke, "I'm sorry for your trouble. You never done me any harm."

Rose assured him that she would not hold a grudge. And that the Irish were famous for holding a grudge and if you were the person they were holding a grudge against, no good would ever come to you. Rose thought that he wasn't a bad looking fellow. He could have polished his style by toning it down a little. One thing that got her attention was a tiny ring on his tiniest finger. She had never seen a man wearing a pinky ring and she had to admit she found herself admiring it and wishing the ring was hers.

In times of peril, the Irish like to talk, so talk Rose did. She told the man her life story and when she finished, he told Rose his. He told her of his parent's immigration to America from a small town near Naples, how he hated school and how he became a street brawler.

Rose asked the I-talian what his name was. She hadn't caught it with all of the commotion. He said most people called him Al but those close to him called him by his given name, Alphonse.

Rose commented, "No one in Ireland has ever been named Alphonse, but I think it tis a lovely name, and one that suits you."

Al replied that he thought the Irish had the funniest names, always putting O's in front of them.

She told Al that if she lived through this, she would cook him an Irish meal. Al had never tasted Irish cooking; only heard the stories about it. He told Rose that he lived in Chicago and probably wouldn't be coming back to Brooklyn in the near future.

Now Simon was sittin' at home, wondering where Rose could be. Paddy and Michael had not seen hide-nor-hair of her since coming from school. When suddenly there was a knock on the door and Simon got up, but when he opened the door no one was there, only a white envelope with Simons name in big red letters. There was a note inside the envelope, it was short and to the point.

*Rose will be dead,*
*dead as dead can be*
*if you don't return our*
*money by the stroke of eight*

There was a map of where he was to go.

Simon knew this was no Irish riddle. He knew what it meant and he knew it was a serious matter. There was another knock on the door. Simon opened the door to find Sgt. O'Reilly.

"Simon, I'm here to have dinner with the most beautiful lassie on the block."

"Sergeant, she's not home yet and running very late. I'm a bit worried."

"Oh, I wouldn't worry if I was you; Rose strikes me as a woman that can hold her own. I'll just sit down here if you don't mind and wait for her."

Simon was in a pickle. He loved his niece and was grateful to her for keeping his home and his business running smooth as silk. It was through no fault of hers that he had become a common criminal. Simon's face began to get milky white and before you could utter Simon's favorite Irish saying—*Choose your company before you sit down*—Simon fainted.

Sgt. O'Reilly had delivered babies, shot at thugs from time-to-time, but never had witnessed a grown man faint.

"Simon, Simon, speak to me."

"God have mercy on me soul, I've done a dirty deed, and Rose will pay the price. Sgt. O'Reilly, you must help me, and then you can arrest me. I've been bringing in the water of life to most of Brooklyn and charging a small fee. I got a bit greedy and was slow with the flow but not with the hand."

"Simon, what the hell are ya talk'n about? Do you work for the Brooklyn Public Works Department?"

"No, no, no, the water of life, sergeant, the water of life, whiskey!"

"Oh no, oh no, no, Simon, it can't be true, right before me eyes. Not you, not the uncle of the woman I'll call me wife some day."

"You'll be scraping her up from the pavement if we don't get to her by the stroke of eight."

Simon told Sgt. O'Reilly his sordid tale and retrieved all of the money that he hid throughout his grand house. Sgt. O'Reilly told Simon he would handle this, meet with Shaun and the I-talian, give the money back and bring Rose safely home.

Sgt. O'Reilly was large in stature, well over six feet with no fat on his bones to speak of. He was a kind man, but no one would ever have known it to meet him. The sight of him caused many a fellow to confess his sins. Sgt. O'Reilly took the money, changed his clothes, borrowed Simon's car and off he went to meet Shaun.

It was getting late and just as Shaun was wondering if Simon would show, Simon's car pulled by the side of the building. No one got out of the car, so Shaun walked over to see what he could see. Just then Sgt. O'Reilly jumped out of the car, grabbed Shaun and put a cold piece to his neck.

"Shaun O'Leary, what would your mother think if her favorite son met with an untimely death, on level ground no less?"

"Sgt. O'Reilly, please, please, please, don't kill me. I'm only doing what I was paid to do"

"Well, Shaun, now you're doing what you're doing because the woman I love is no trapeze artist and needs to come down and go home to be with her lads."

Shaun took Sgt. O'Reilly up in the lift all the way to the 21st floor. When they got there, they saw the I-talian sitting in front of Rose, shoes off, feet hanging over the edge, oblivious of anyone around. And there was Rose, talking softly, almost a whispering voice. Sgt. O'Reilly listened hard. He thought she was reciting a verse from Yates because that was her favorite Irish poet. But Sgt. O'Reilly had never heard this verse before.

"I am still of opinion that only two topics can be of interest to a serious mood such as this, and those two topics are sex and the dead."

Sgt. O'Reilly was not about to listen to another word. He stepped right in, pointed the gun at the I-talian, untied Rose, and took the lot of them down the lift and got Rose home to safety.

I'm pleased to tell you the truth; there's a happy ending to a bit of a mucked-up situation. The I-talian went back to Chicago. Shaun never again behaved in such a brazen way. All those concerned got their money back. Simon didn't go to jail. Rose married Sgt. O'Reilly.

And I'll tell you a secret. Well, it's no secret if three people know it, and there's more than three of you here. This secret is not known to a living soul, not a living breathing soul, that Rose Mulligan O'Reilly kept a tiny ring tucked deep in the folds beneath her pillow, kept it there for all the remaining days of her glorious life.

# Don't Run For The Priest After The Patient Has Died

It was a cold winter day in Brooklyn and Rose Mulligan was not at her best. She had been suffering from the croup over the last several months. She was a long way from her place of birth, Dublin, Ireland. And she felt today might just be the day she would go to meet her maker. Rose, a widow twice, was a healthy lass for most of her 80 years. There's an Irish saying—*He who is dying every day will live the longest.* If you had listened to Rose over the last 80 years, every day was going to be her last. Of course, Rose was brought up in Ireland where her mother, grandmother and aunt told her every time she coughed, "sickness begins with a cough and ends with a coffin."

Poor Rose took those words with her when she came to live in America. Dr. Patrick

Keegan was Rose's doctor since she arrived in Brooklyn with her two small lads. Rose was his best patient. Not that she was brave and didn't yell or complain when she got a shot. No, she was his best patient because she went to see him every week, with this-that-and every-thing, and the good doctor made a tidy living from Rose's ailments. Now, Dr. Keegan had his standard line each time Rose paid a visit, "a good laugh and a long sleep are the best cures."

This day, Rose was truly feeling that the tide was coming in and she was going out. She called her oldest son Michael and told him this was the day, to come quickly and to ask Monsignor O'Neill to give her the last rites.

Now, Michael lived in Manhattan, a stone's throw from Brooklyn, and he did as she asked. Manhattan's lifestyle was a world apart from Brooklyn. Michael had lived in Manhattan for many years, highly successful in the advertising world of snappy patter. He had never arranged for anyone to receive the last rites and was not sure how it all went.

He called upon his wife Katherine to come with him to his mother's home. Katherine was not Irish and worse yet, Rose referred to her as The Protestant. Indeed, Katherine was not Catholic and it was a bit of a disappointment to Rose that Michael couldn't find one of his own to marry. But if truth be known, Rose loved Katherine and Katherine loved Rose.

Michael and Katherine arrived at Rose's home and Monsignor O'Neill was notified to come and give Rose the last rites. The monsignor's last words to Michael before he hung up the telephone were, "Please start the preparations and I'll be there as soon as I can."

What preparations? Michael didn't have a clue, so Michael's youngest cousin, Meghan Kennedy who lived a few blocks away, came to the house to assist. Meghan was only sixteen but knew her catechism backwards and forwards and was sure to be of great help. Meghan was pleased as punch that Michael and Katherine had such confidence in her. She began to give instructions like a member of the Irish Republic Army: "Close all of the drapes, do it now, do not let one ray of light in, this is very important."

Rose's house was a two-story brownstone with windows that reached almost from the floor to the ceiling. All of the window drapes with the exception of the kitchen and bathroom were velvet and pulled to each side. Katherine had a terrible time closing them, they were so heavy, and it took all of her might.

"Go get the holy water. Leave it at the table beside Rose's bed; do it now, this is very important."

Michael found it hard to believe—it appeared there was not a drop of holy water in the house—truly unheard of. When he was growing up it seemed like there were buckets full. His mother would say, "When there's holy water in the home, the devil flies out the window."

Michael shouted out to Katherine, "Katherine, I can't find the holy water."

Katherine with all her dignity and class replied, "Michael, I am sure as Hell not going to St. Patrick's to bottle up some of their holy water."

As luck would have it, Michael looked in his mother's medicine cabinet and came running out. "I've found it. I've found it, a tiny bottle by God, marked holy water!"

Katherine gave Michael that look, the I-don't-believe-you look.

"No, no, it's true Katherine, this is holy water. I'd be afraid to lie about anything with the word 'holy' in it. Mom always says, "You can go across the bridge to that high-falutin' place, Manhattan, where there's fancy restaurants and shops, but remember Michael, even the best of them will eventually close, but Hell, Hell is always open."

Meghan continued with the orders, "Turn all of the lights off in the house, do it now, this is very important." Michael and Katherine went all around the house turning out every light.

Michael asked, "Well, Meghan, what do we do now?"

"We wait for Monsignor O'Neill and I'll greet him at the door with one lit candle."

The hours came and went. It was getting rather dark outside and inside. Michael got the flashlight from his car so they could at least see where the Hell they were walking. Meghan stood as the watchman peeking out the window looking for Monsignor O'Neill. A bright yellow MG pulled in front of the house. A tall gentleman with a Doctor Zhivago coat and hat got out of the car.

Meghan gasped, "It's not Monsignor O'Neill. It's Father Walenski, the new and very young priest at Saint Patrick's. Oh my God, he's so beautiful; I can't let him see me like this."

"Meghan, where the Hell is Monsignor O'Neill? And what do you mean you can't let him see you like this? You are the one that's going to greet him at the door with the candle."

"No, no, Cousin Michael, I'm too embarrassed."

Katherine with all her dignity and class shouted out, "Michael, I am sure as Hell not going to the door in the damn dark with this candle."

Michael was never at a loss for words. He did work on Madison Avenue where you don't have to be Irish to know it's a wise thing to always have a few words on the tip of your tongue. There were none that day. He reached for the candle, lit it, and walked to the front door to greet the father.

"Hi, I'm Father Walenski. Monsignor O'Neill sends his regrets. He simply couldn't make it. May I ask why it's so dark in your house? I looked up and saw not one light on and thought perhaps no one was home. I see you have a candle, did the electricity go out?"

There is an Irish saying—*Crying is not far away from laughter.*

"Father, I'm going to tell you the truth. We thought—we, my cousin Meghan, a young, good Catholic girl; my wife Katherine, a Protestant; and myself, yes, myself, which is hard for me to believe right now—that this was the procedure followed in preparation for my mother to receive the last rites."

"Michael, perhaps in a Eugene O'Neill play the scene might look a bit like this, but on Prospect Park West among all these fine houses, it is a shame that we can't see each other to know who is dying, and who isn't. Believe me, Michael, the Catholic Church has come a long way. Please blow out the candle and turn all of the lights back on."

Father Walenski introduced himself to Katherine and gave a warm hello to Meghan. There was much concern among the group as to who was going to tell Rose that Monsignor O'Neill sent his regrets. Katherine, with all her dignity and class said, "Michael, it sure as Hell isn't going to be me."

Father Walenski assured them he did not have a problem with simply going into Rose's bedroom alone, introducing himself, and giving her the last rites.

Michael was not at a loss for words now.

"Well, father, if you don't have a problem going it alone, be our guest."

Rose was lying in the bed, one eye closed, one eye opened. She looked at the tall young man wearing the white collar coming through the door.

"I am so grateful to serve you, Mrs. Mulligan. I'm Father Walenski from Saint Patrick's. I've come in place of Monsignor O'Neill."

"Come in place of the monsignor? Where might he be?"

"Monsignor O'Neill sent his regrets, he simply couldn't make it."

"Simply couldn't make it, with me on me death bed, has he no shame? You can't make a piano out of a bacon box."

"I've never thought of the monsignor as a bacon box, but he certainly can eat a lot of it. Mrs. Mulligan, I believe I am qualified to comfort you and to administer the last rites if it is your desire for me to do so. You remind me of my mother, sweet, gentle and kind."

"You don't say—sweet, gentle and kind. What part of Ireland does she come from?"

"She didn't come from Ireland, she came from Poland and she died last year."

"Do you have any brothers and sisters?"

"No. I am an only child."

"Now that's a pity, so it's only you and Monsignor What's-His-Name?"

"Mrs. Mulligan, I am blessed to have all of God's people as my family. And I'm so pleased that I am here with you today. Tell me a little about yourself and your family."

There is an Irish saying—*Good humor comes from the kitchen*. I'm here to tell you, there was no humor coming from the kitchen that day. Michael, Katherine and Meghan were all huddled there waiting for hours and starving to death. They could not imagine what was taking so long.

Actually, Katherine was becoming concerned and spoke up, "Michael, far be it for me to tell you what to do, but one of us needs to go into your mother's bedroom to see what the Hell is going on."

The Irish say—*Marriages are all happy; it's the having breakfast together that causes the problems*. Michael thought they'd all be having breakfast together if someone didn't do something soon, but he didn't say a word.

Katherine, with all her class and dignity, said, "OK, OK, damn it, Michael. I'll be the one to go. And if I don't come out in a timely manner, please, please, pay me the respect to come and check on me."

Michael never really thought about it over the last several hours, knowing his mother, anything is possible. She could have murdered the father and be looking for a place in her bedroom to bury him.

Katherine entered Rose's bedroom to find Rose asleep. Katherine knew she was asleep because Rose was snoring. Father Walenski was sitting on the bed holding Rose's hand.

"Katherine, your mother-in-law is quite a storyteller. I have enjoyed the last two hours and twenty-four minutes! When it's Rose's time, she will be ready, thanks to all of you. You did the right thing. In my country, Poland, we have a saying—*Don't run for the priest after the patient has died*.

Rose lived for another two years and when she was on her deathbed Monsignor O'Neill was, indeed, at her side.

# God Bless You, Rose Mulligan

Rose Mulligan died on September 9, 1970, and was laid out at Malloy's Funeral Home in Brooklyn. It was going to be a grand time. Two days at Malloy's, a funeral mass at Saint Patrick's, then on to the place of rest and, last but not least, the wake at Flanagan's Bar & Grill. Rose had been planning for this celebration since her birth. She gave complete instructions to the daughter-in-law she trusted, Katherine, who was the only Protestant in Rose's family. "The other one," as Rose referred to Mary Gallagher, her Catholic daughter-in-law, never took any of Rose's guff or advice.

Rose once told Mary when Mary was courting her youngest son Patrick, "Don't marry me boy Patrick. You'll ruin his life."

Rose freely gave advice to Patrick regarding women and Mary in particular,

"Never run after a bus or a woman named Mary. There will always be another one along in a few minutes."

As fate would have it, Mary and Patrick eloped and moved far away to California. It was well known in the family that Rose and Mary never spoke well of one another.

Several years before Rose died she and Katherine went shopping to buy a dress for Rose to wear in her coffin. It was an interesting day for Katherine, one she will not forget. Each shop they entered, Katherine would say, "We're looking for the perfect dress for Mrs. Mulligan, my mother-in-law, something that will go with her complexion, not too flashy and not too blah. A dress everyone present will remember."

All of the shopkeepers did their best searching for the perfect dress until they inquired, "Mrs. Mulligan, exactly where will you be wearing this dress?"

"I'll be wearin' it in me coffin."

They seemed to lose interest and urged Mrs. Mulligan to try elsewhere. Only Hymie Goldberg, a good friend of Rose's and owner of Fine Women's Apparel, understood and found her the perfect pink dress. Rose loved the color pink but never had the courage to wear it.

Hymie reassured her, "Rose if you are brave enough to die, you're brave enough to wear pink."

He also talked Rose into buying pink shoes to go with the dress. The shoes were a half-size smaller than Rose usually wore but, as Hymie put it, "a little pinch in the toes isn't going to bother you."

The time had come to pass. Rose was in the grandest room at Malloy's Funeral Home in her pink dress not looking a minute older than eight-two. Malloy's was full-to-the brim with those that had died, those that had come to mourn and those that were hoping to be asked to a wake for a bit of liquid refreshment. It was an interesting day for Katherine, one she will not forget. She had never seen so many flower arrangements. Michael, Katherine's husband and Rose's oldest son, said the Irish were keen on sending flowers to the funeral home. The flowers were placed in relationship to the sender's standing with the deceased. Uncle Connor, one of Rose's favorite relatives, was in charge of placing the flowers as they arrived. Uncle Connor's flowers were in the first row, closest to the coffin, along with Cousin Thomas, Cousin Doyle, Cousin Margaret and Cousin John's. Cousin Theresa's flowers were placed in the second row. Theresa had the great misfortune of being the child of Rose's late sister Grace. Uncle Connor was well aware that the two sisters never lit a fire without disagreeing.

Katherine thought at first she was imagining that the flower arrangements were moving. That was not the case. They were. As soon as Uncle Connor left the room, the flowers in row two quickly moved up to row one. In Irish families, reverence ceases once blood is spilled. Barely a petal was left on any of the flowers that day. They moved around more than a goalie tending the goal.

Quarreling among relatives is a national pastime for the Irish and something Mr. Malloy, the undertaker, handled well. "If you don't stop now, I'll have the lot of you arrested and there'll not be a drop given out for your grief."

The next morning was glorious, perfect for the celebration of the funeral mass. It was another interesting day for Katherine, and one she will not forget. It was just as Rose had planned it. Monsignor O'Neill presided over the mass. Everyone who spoke only gave words of praise. Michael gave the eulogy. He was magnificent. Rose wrote every word of it and spent years helping Michael with the delivery, right down to the hand gestures. Rose really was hoping Peter O'Toole would be alive when she died so he could give the eulogy but Michael reminded her that Peter wasn't related to them and his fee would be a bit more than they could afford.

The cemetery was not located in Brooklyn and somewhat of a journey. Two limousines were lined up outside the church to transport the close relatives. Rose gave specific instructions to Katherine in regard to who was going to ride in a limousine and in which order. Katherine did not want to let Rose down. She parked herself in front of limousine number one.

"Connor, Thomas, Margaret, John, Michael, Patrick, and Doyle, you will be riding in limousine number one. Shannon, Meghan, Kevin, Jack, Dillon, Kathleen, and Brian, you will be riding in limousine number two."

No one made a move; they were all still standing at the curb. Some were stunned—why should they be riding in limousine number two, did Rose love them less than those riding in number one? Mary, Patrick's wife, had not had her name called. It wasn't that Katherine had forgotten her. It was part of Rose's instructions to simply give Mary the handwritten directions how to get to the cemetery in Staten Island by bus and ferry.

But Katherine simply couldn't do it. She decided to take matters into her own hands and in the most caring voice she could muster up, she said, "Mary, Rose loved you the most, even though she didn't show it. You are the one she honored to ride in Monsignor O'Neill's car."

There was a long pause, then Mary gave Katherine a wink, and muttered softly before grabbing the Monsignor's arm, "For your sake, Rose, I hope the devil is kind to his own!"

Ashes to ashes, and dust to dust, it was almost over. They were all headed back to Brooklyn to Flanagan's Bar & Grill for the wake. It was an interesting day for Katherine, and one she will not forget. All those that were living and were anybody in Prospect Park West in Brooklyn were at Flanagan's that afternoon.

Flanagan stood on a table and announced,

"A blessing feeds no one, so grab a plate and fill your glass. Remember, it's the first drop that will destroy you so there's no harm at all in the last."

There were two kinds of Irish whiskey, John Jameson for the Catholics and the Democrats and Bushmill's for the Protestants and the Republicans; Guinness for the blue collars and red wine for the I-talians. Joey Gallino and his brothers came to pay their respect. Rose enjoyed their company. She fed them breakfast every now and then when they weren't in jail or taking to their mattresses.

Michael would warn her, "Mom, you're the one that always said, a good name is easier lost than gained."

Rose would simply reply, "Oh, Michael, pay the newspapers no mind, they're good lads. What kills one man gives life to another."

Hymie Goldberg was roaming through the crowd looking for something to eat. On one table, hot out of the oven, was the baked ham. Over at another table, was the cold sliced ham. Just as he was about to give up, Flanagan himself came over.

"Hymie, Rose made me promise to feed you right."

And as sure as you can say, "You don't know what's in the pot until the lid is lifted," there it was, a big pot of matzohball soup.

Brian Cavanaugh the neighborhood butcher joined Hymie tasting a bit of the soup and loving every spoonful.

Hymie asked Brain, "What did you think of Rose's dress?"

"What dress, Hymie?"

"The one she was wearing in her coffin."

"To tell you the truth, Hymie, I never like to look inside the coffins. I'm dealing with dead meat every day."

Thomas Sullivan overhead their conversation. "Hymie, the pink dress was lovely and just perfect for Rose."

Mr. Sullivan was a prominent defense attorney for those that could afford him, and the best dressed of the lot, other than Rose herself.

As Rose would say, "A sly rogue is often well-dressed."

Mr. Sullivan had a way with the ladies. He had a wife in his grand house on Prospect Park West and it was rumored that he kept a mistress on the Upper Eastside of Manhattan. Rose could never understand where he found the time or the energy, as the Irish say—*Too much of one thing is the same thing as nothing*.

Deidre Duffy, Rose's neighbor, entered into the conversation. "Pink dress did you say? I never did get to see it. Those damn flowers were blockin' me view."

Long as the day may be, the night comes at last and thank goodness. The bloom on Rose's wake was beginning to fade and so was Katherine. It was almost time to go home. Rose had given Katherine the final instructions to have her two favorite neighbors speak the last elegant words as Flanagan's closed the door.

James Houlihan stepped up, lifted his glass and said, "Rose had a good run and that's better than a bad stand. Let's all drink to that."

And Brady McGuire, a man of few words and great wisdom, shouted out, "We live as long as we're let, except for Rose, who lived life on her own terms, for as long as she saw fit! God Bless ya, Rose Mulligan."

# The Devil Never Took A Good Heart To Hell

Rose O'Brien was the only child of
Lionel and Mary O'Brien. Her parents came
from Dublin in the late 1940s and settled in
Brooklyn where Rose was born. The family
lived above Lionel's place of business. Most
of the people in Rose's neighborhood were
Irish or of Irish decent so Rose spoke with a
bit of a brogue. She had no knowledge of other
nationalities to speak of. All the tradesmen that
delivered goods to her father's business were
Irish. All of her father's patrons were Irish. All
the people that went to mass at Saint Savior's
were Irish. Not to mention that all of the lads
that came courting Rose were Irish. Rose knew
more about Ireland and Irish ways than any
Irish born Irishman. She sang like a bird and
was the apple of her father's eye. He so loved
to have her by his side and taught her the tricks
of his trade. Rose loved her father almost as

much as she loved God.

When Rose became a lass of 18 and was getting ready to be graduated, she made an announcement. Rose told Lionel and Mary she wanted to serve God for the rest of her life. She wanted to become a nun.

Now, Rose had never been out of Brooklyn. Never even went across the bridge into the big city, Manhattan by name. You can only imagine the fear that came upon her when she learned she was going to be sent to a convent in Texas. Texas is famous by all Irish standards. Texans are great storytellers; they've been known to stretch the truth; they have a high opinion of themselves; they get a bit rowdy once in a while; and they like to eat good solid stick-to-your ribs food. From all she had seen on the telly and read in books, her only hope to survive in Texas was the fact that Hopalong Cassidy and Roy Rogers lived there and they would protect her.

Rose shared a tiny room in the convent with one other nun, Sister Rita. Sister Rita grew up in a small Texas town called Cut-And-Shoot. She could ride like the wind, shoot straight as an arrow and was quite the Texas Two-Stepper. She taught Rose the ins and outs of being a

Texan. She told her God loved Texas better than any other of the states, and that most Texans were lucky and rich. As the years went by Rose began to think more and more like a Texan. Between the prayer and her newly acquired Texan confidence there was no task she couldn't tackle.

One day Rose received a letter that her father's business was doing very poorly. Since her mother died, Lionel O'Brien lost a bit of his spirit and so did his business. There were only a few customers that were loyal to Lionel. Before long he was going to lose it all. Rose told Sister Rita she longed to go home and help her father. Ah, they knew that was not possible. Mother Superior would not allow Rose to return to Brooklyn if she knew the truth. The only answer was to fib.

Rose told Mother Superior that her father was not well and his grocery store, yes, his grocery store, was going to close. She told Mother Superior that her father was not ordering enough milk for the wee ones and the mums couldn't buy fruits and vegetables for their families. He was letting the store go to, well, Hell. She asked Mother Superior for a leave of absence to go to Brooklyn to tend to her family matters. Mother Superior gave her consent but on the condition that two chaperones would go along. Sister Rita would accompany Rose at all times and Father Travis McGuire would join them to offer support if needed.

Now Father McGuire did not have a church of his own. He was ordered by the Texas Diocese to give the convent his assistance as needed. Sister Rita was not a fan of Father McGuire and as she put it, "a dumb priest never got a parish." There was no choice. The three of them left for Brooklyn.

There is an Irish saying—*The man who has luck in the morning has luck in the afternoon.* This is certainly the case with Rose. When the three arrived in Brooklyn the morning of March 10th, Rose and Sister Rita were lodged at the Rectory of Saint Savior's, very close to Rose's father's grocery store. Yes, his grocery store. Much to their joy there was no room for Father McGuire at Saint Savior's rectory. Later that afternoon, Father McGuire was taken to Saint Patrick's, miles from the grocery store. Yes, miles from the grocery store. Rose and Sister Rita could not believe their good fortune to learn the priest at Saint Patrick's had more parishioners than he could handle and he had asked for Father McGuire's help in celebrating seven funerals that were scheduled that week.

Now, Sister Rita knew all there was to know about Rose and her life in Brooklyn. She had to admit to herself that she would fantasize about Rose's girlhood years while sweeping the convent kitchen floor. Not a good thing to be thinking of if you're a nun, but then again, there is an Irish saying—*A good sweep of the kitchen is as good as a prayer.*

Rose was off to see her father with Sister Rita tagging along looking every which way through the streets of Brooklyn. She had never seen so many people walking the streets in her life. Where she grew up in Texas, you had to go miles and miles before you saw a soul.

They arrived at Rose's father's place of business. Sister Rita looked up and it was just as she had imagined: a big green sign with bold letters:

# O'BRIEN'S BAR & GRILL

There was one small sentence written underneath the name:

*What Whiskey Won't Cure,*
*There's No Cure For*

Sister Rita so wanted to have her picture taken in front of that sign to take back to show the other sisters to have a laugh on a day when no laugh was to be found.

Rose rushed inside and there was Lionel O'Brien sitting by himself. It was five o'clock in the afternoon, things should be bustling with tables and the bar being cleaned and the Dublin pot pies and the corned beef in the oven. There were not even bowls of pretzels on the bar. She hugged her father and listened to his tale of woe.

All of the lads that came to O'Brien's Bar for years and years told Lionel he had lost his will to live and O'Brien's had become a dull place to be. *An Irishman's wit is on his tongue* is a saying as old as the green hills of Ireland. Silence is golden, but not in a bar. Lionel was no longer witty, his whiskey was weak, the food was cold and there was no music to be heard in the place since Rose left and her mum died.

Now, Rose was quite the entertainer at O'Brien's. She sang all of the Irish tunes every Friday and Saturday night. She knew the words from the time she was knee-high to a grasshopper. Every Irish lad and lassie knew the rebel songs before they could recite the Lord's Prayer. Some just carried a tune better than others. Rose could certainly carry a tune, her mum played the piano and a grand time was had by all. Lionel's patrons had deserted him and gave their business to Fiona Foley's pub. Now, beauty doesn't boil the pot and Fiona was a bit hard to look at, but there was laughter at her place.

Sister Rita overheard their conversation. She put her two cents in, "It's time for a change and many a sudden change takes place in a spring day."

It wasn't spring yet but it was almost Saint Patrick's Day and that's spring, Christmas and Easter all rolled into one.

"You're a handsome man, Mr. O'Brien, and smart, too. Your place, even your sign, is just perfect. Rose tells me your pot pies are the best in Brooklyn, maybe even better than those in Texas. Your wife is dead, Mr. O'Brien, you're not. Your wife would want you to carry on with O'Brien's. Make people laugh, make them sing and, yes, let them drink!

"All of Brooklyn would go to mass every morning if holy water were whiskey!"

Rose and Sister Rita returned to the Rectory

of Saint Savior's to pray for wisdom to help Mr. O'Brien. It became clear to Rose that her father was a lonely man. After all, her mum used to say, "A man without a woman is like a neck without a pain."

There was a woman Rose remembered from her childhood that had hair as red as fire with a laugh so loud and smile so broad she made all around her happy. She could sing, not as fine as Rose, but every now and then she would come to O'Brien's with her husband and sing a ditty or two.

Rose thought her name was Grace O'Rourke and that her husband had died. Rose asked the cook at the Rectory if Grace O'Rourke still lived in the neighborhood.

"Yes, yes, she does, sister. She is a widow and doesn't get out much."

Rose thought what a silly question she asked. Of course, Grace O'Rourke still lived in the neighborhood. Everyone does except those that are taken out in a box or enter a convent.

Rose began to reminiscence about her youth. She told Sister Rita how much she loved the time spent in her father's bar singing the tunes. O'Brien's was full of life. She thought the customers came for the music more than they came for the whiskey.

"That's the answer, Sister Rita. We must bring back the music and they will come."

Rose telephoned Grace O'Rourke and the rest of the story is a sight to behold.

Three women in a pub, two women in a habit, one woman with long red hair down to her waist all singing like they were the female version of the Clancy Brothers: *Whiskey, You're the Devil, The Pub with no Beer, Water is Alright in Tay.* Irish drinking songs to be sure. Never done better by God. That's what most of the patrons said that night, Saint Patrick's night, the opening night of the new

# O'BRIEN'S BAR & GRILL

Rose, Sister Rita and Father McGuire went back to Texas. Father McGuire complaining all the way. He never got to meet Rose's father and never got to visit the grocery store. He was so busy, as he put it, "with those damn funerals!"

Grace O'Rourke stayed at the pub and sang her heart out every Friday and Saturday night and eventually gave her heart to Mr. O'Brien.

It is told in Brooklyn, to this day, that

# O'BRIEN'S BAR & GRILL

is packed to the gills every night and it's the only pub in Brooklyn where on Saint Patrick's night, the closing tune is *Cotton Eye Joe*.

Thanks be to God, Sister Rita.

# Your Feet Will Take You To Where Your Heart Is

Rose Breslin was raised in Brooklyn from the time she was 12 years of age. Her parents, Ryan and Colleen Breslin, emigrated to America from County Cork, Ireland, in the early 1950s. They felt at home in Brooklyn among the Irish families in their neighborhood. Rose was a daring young lass who was never afraid to speak her mind. She turned many a young man's head with her long flowing red hair, green eyes and skin as smooth as a silk purse. The only flaw Rose had was located between her knees and her feet. She had no ankles to speak of. Whenever Rose complained about her legs, her mother would say, "Hush. You should get on your knees and thank God that your were born with feet and forget what's between them."

It's the Irish girls' curse to be born with legs thick as beams. The Italian boys on the block often joked that if the Brooklyn Bridge was falling down, the best bet to keep it from collapsing would be a bunch of Irish girls standing under it.

Rose had always wanted to be a ballroom dancer but never danced a step because she was ashamed of "those damned piano legs!"

One Sunday afternoon, Rose was reading the *Brooklyn Eagle* and saw an advertisement for ballroom dancing lessons given at the Knights of Columbus Hall. She wanted to dance more than anything else. Even more than her endless desire to kiss her boss, Thomas Donovan, the manager of the Brooklyn Dime Savings Bank. Much to Rose's distress, Mr. Donovan never so much as gave her a glance. It was only Rose's vanity and the fact that Mr. Donovan could fire her that prevented the thoughts in her head from being played out on the floor of the most fashionable bank in Brooklyn.

Rose mustered up the courage to learn ballroom dancing in spite of her legs. She asked her parents if she could sign up for the lessons. Ryan and Colleen thought it was a grand idea. Rose was sure to meet a good Catholic lad.

After work on Monday evening, Rose went to the Hall and had her first dancing lesson. Mr. David Kaplan, a shopkeeper by trade, was her instructor. Mr. Kaplan was a striking gentleman who was at least six feet tall with dark curly hair. He glided along the floor as though he was on a cloud. Rose was impressed and paid close attention to his instructions.

"Rose, keep your head up. Look me straight in the eye and hold your body close to mine. Pretend you and I are the only people on earth. There's no one else here Rose, no one— not even the Pope."

Rose blushed but felt bold enough to add, "Mr. Kaplan, the Pope may not be here but the Virgin Mary, who is around my neck, is sure to feel your chest leaning against her gold chain. So if you don't mind, the three of us are going to learn the fox trot."

Four evenings a week Rose took her dance lessons. After several months there was no question Rose was the best in the class. She was certain Mr. Kaplan would ask her to participate in the ballroom dancing competition held at Roseland in Manhattan. Sure as fate, Mr. Kaplan walked over to Rose and announced to the class.

"I've selected Miss Rose Breslin to be my dance partner for the fox trot competition at Roseland next Saturday evening."

Mr. Kaplan told Rose she would have to purchase a dress for the occasion.

"Rose, I want you to wear a long black dress, one without a slit up the side. And please, leave Mary at home. A simple string of pearls will do."

Colleen and Ryan were so proud of their daughter. Many of the Irish girls in the neighborhood step-danced at school and church recitals. But none ever performed in Manhattan. Paddy Scully, a New York City Transit conductor, and a friend of the Breslins, mapped out the subway route to Roseland. And so it was, the Irish contingent made up of the Fitzgeralds, the Farrells, the Dunns, the O'Connors, the McClures, the Moynihans and the McCormacks sat ring-side at Roseland to see Rose Breslin perform. They couldn't believe their eyes. They were disturbing the spectators with all of their enthusiasm and Irish pride.

"Oh, Colleen, your daughter's a vision," Joe Farrell blurted out for all to hear. "It's plain to see, it's to the glory of Ireland that she dances. For sure, the next step for Rose is the Radio City Music Hall."

Mr. Fitzgerald, the oldest of the group, stood on his feet and cheered. "If only the Irish Army were here to see her."

Ryan Breslin himself got a bit carried away and shouted, "If Saint Patrick was here, he'd marry her."

When Mr. Kaplan and Rose won first prize in the fox trot competition, the lot of them, stood-up and cheered, "Ireland Forever!"

Rose was a bit embarrassed. Mr. Kaplan gave her a look. But she stood her ground. "It's my ancestry! You should celebrate, too, Mr. Kaplan. Let your people go, Mr. Kaplan. Let your people go with my people!"

And so he did. Mr. Kaplan's mother and father, Esther and Morris, and his three brothers joined in the celebration. The evening ended at Katz's delicatessen with pastrami sandwiches and egg creams for all.

Rose was the best dance student Mr. Kaplan ever had. She mastered the Viennese waltz, the fox trot and the rumba. Each time there was a dance competition, Mr. Kaplan would select Rose as his partner. Each time, he would counsel Rose on what to wear.

"For the waltz, Rose, purchase a full skirt and make sure it goes all the way to the floor. And for the rumba, Rose, it must be a leopard skin dress down to your ankles."

Rose and Mr. Kaplan always won the fox trot and waltz competitions. They became the darlings of the ballroom circuit. Both the *Irish Free Press* and the *Jewish Herald* carried stories of their success. They were sure to be picked by the judges for the Harvest Moon Ball competition held at Madison Square Garden. Winning the Harvest Moon was to a ballroom dancer what the winning of the Nobel Prize for Literature was to an Irishman.

Rose's confidence had reached an all time high. As her mother put it, "Rose's so full of herself, she can't fit through the front door."

Rose knew enough about the Harvest Moon competition to know it was the tango that could make or break you. The tango was by far her favorite dance and one she excelled in. No Irish lass had ever won a tango competition in New York City. Rose called upon her friend, Maggie McFadden, who owned Ireland's Own Beauty Parlor, to help her acquire the look of a vamp. Maggie pulled Rose's hair back tightly to form a bun. She curled two hairs one on each side of Rose's head and let them hang down her neck. Maggie placed large gold hoops on Rose's ears. She turned her eyebrows and eyelids into a mass of long thick black strokes. When Maggie finished with Rose she paraded her into Tim Finnegan's Pub for all of the patrons to give her a look. They placed Rose on top of the bar where she proceeded to execute the most perfect fan and corte. Tim Finnegan smiled and his one sentence said it all, "Carmen, please save the last tango for me."

Rose had the steps down pat and now she had the look. She could hardly wait for her next dance lesson to tell David she was ready to enter a tango competition. That evening at the Hall, Mr. Kaplan and Rose were once again practicing the fox trot routine. Rose was getting bored with the slow-dancin' and spoke up. "If I must say it myself, I am the best tango dancer in Brooklyn."

"I'm sure you are, Rose. Chita Lopez is the best tango dancer in New York City and Rosa Rivera and Maria Casa are not far behind her."

"Mr. Kaplan, if you're concerned that I look too Irish to dance the tango and win, then you are gravely, gravely mistaken."

"Rose, did I hear you say gravely, gravely mistaken?"

"Oh, Mr. Kaplan, I'm sorry. It's my Irish upbringing; too many Irish rebellion stories. But Mr. Kaplan, you know in your heart I can do it."

"It's true, Miss Breslin, I do know in my heart you can do it but as a professional dancer and one who truly wants to win the Harvest Moon tango competition, I'm not going to allow you to compete."

"What reason could there be, Mr. Kaplan, what reason could there be? I've gotten my dress and it's just perfect. The first dress I've ever picked without you. Wait right here, I'll put it on."

Rose came out in a short, black, sequined dress that was right above her knees.

"Look, Mr. Kaplan, I think the short dress is just right for the tango. Don't you think I look terrific?"

Silence is often the same as the truth in many cultures, so Mr. Kaplan thought he had better set it right.

"Rose, this is hard for me to say, but it must be said. You have Irish legs; you can't dance a tango without ankles!"

Rose ran out of the Hall before Mr. Kaplan could comfort her. She ran through the streets of Brooklyn as though bullets were flying from the guns of the IRA. She was running so fast that she knocked Thomas Donovan, who was just locking the bank doors, straight down, smack on the sidewalk. Rose fell on top of him with her legs spread out near his. She still had on the short dress and tried to cover her legs with her scarf.

"Miss Breslin, there's no need for you to try and cover your legs. I've been looking at them for some time now, almost from your first day at the bank. You have beautiful legs, Miss Breslin."

There is an Irish saying—*There's no cure for sorrow but to put it underfoot.*

And that's exactly what Rose did. She pulled Mr. Donovan's face to hers and gave him a kiss to remember. Mr. Donovan helped Rose up and walked her home holding her hand tightly in his.

# A Bit Of A Stretch

Rose Kelley was a happily married Irish woman with grown children. Rose, her husband John, and their two daughters were born in Dublin. In the early 1950s they decided to come to American and live in Brooklyn with other family members. As Rose grew older she was becoming a bit bored with her life even though she kept busy as a member of Saint Patrick's Altar Guild, the Women's Bible Study and baby-sat her grandchildren every now and then. John made a good wage. He owned his own insurance agency and Rose didn't have to worry about money. Ah, but Rose would complain to John that she felt guilty about having too much time and too much money.

John would tell her, "Rose, it's better to be full of plenty than be on the edge of poverty. You know what you need? You need a hobby. A hobby where there aren't so many church women around. You're the apple of me eye. I want you to be happy. Find something that will put a little color in your cheeks and a little excitement in your life."

Monday's were empty days for Rose. She decided to pay her friend Mrs. O'Grady a visit. Mrs. O'Grady's son Brian was sitting in her kitchen busily reading the newspaper.

"Brian, your head seems to be buried in the *Brooklyn Eagle*. Is there something important we should all know?" Rose asked.

"No, not unless you're going to the track today and looking to put your money on the winning ponies."

"So, Brian, it's the ponies that interest you?"

"Yes, Mrs. Kelley, I do better with them than the women. I like the fresh air; it puts a little color in my cheeks. And I must admit, the excitement of each race can't be beat."

"You don't say. I've never been to the races. They're big in Ireland you know."

"If you're not doing anything today, why don't you come along with me."

"Me, I don't think so. What would Mr. Kelley say?"

"Well, he wouldn't say anything if you didn't tell him."

"Not tell him?"

"Certainly, Mrs. Kelley, you don't tell your husband everything. My mother never has and they both seem quite content with it that way. Surely, Mrs. Kelley, you know the Irish saying—*Pity the woman who tells her husband all of her secrets.*

"No, I can't say I have."

"Come with me, Mrs. Kelley, you'll have a good time."

Desperation often gives courage to a coward and Rose was desperate to breakout of her rut. She smiled and whispered, "If you promise me we'll be back before supper and you won't say a word of this to anyone, I'll go."

"I promise, Mrs. Kelley, I promise."

Brian and Rose arrived at Belmont Race Track slightly before the first race was to begin. Brian quickly took her to the most expensive seats at the track, the box seats, reserved each season by the well-to-do. Already seated were several gentlemen decked out in the likes of finery that Rose had never seen. One rather large man was wearing black and white checked trousers and a yellow handkerchief the size of a scarf bellowing out of his black jacket. His outfit was not a common sight in her neighborhood. Another was dressed in bright green trousers and a royal blue jacket. Rose felt a bit odd. Not only was she dressed in the very dull color of gray, but she was the only woman present.

Brian placed Rose next to a gentleman named William. William appeared to be the most genteel of the group. His sport coat and trousers were made of silk and he wore a red ascot around his neck. William gave Rose his full attention,

"I'm pleased to meet you, Mrs. Kelley. Now, what horse will you be playing in the first race?"

"I didn't come to play the ponies. I only came to get a bit of fresh air to put some color in me cheeks."

"Mrs. Kelley, may I call you Rose?"

"Well, yes, I guess."

"Well, Rose, you'll miss the excitement if you don't participate in the game."

Rose liked the way he spoke. He had authority in his voice.

"Sir, I wouldn't know which horse to pick."

"Please call me William."

"William, I've never been to a race track in me life."

"Then you are sure to have beginners luck. So don't be afraid and take a look at the horses walking toward the gate and select one."

Rose looked the field over. She picked the sorriest looking horse. Brian was a bit embarrassed by Rose's choice and spoke up, "Mrs. Kelley, surely you have heard the Irish saying—*A nod is as good as a wink to a blind horse!*

"No, Brian, I can't say that I have. But I've heard it's often not the best looking horse that wins the race. So I'll go with Number Five."

"Number Five it is for Rose and me. Brian please place our bets."

Brian couldn't believe his ears and was stunned that William gave him two 100-dollar bills to be placed on the nose of Number Five.

As beginner's luck would have it, Number Five was indeed the winner. Rose was a bit surprised that William had trusted her woman's intuition, that the horse actually won and that he insisted on sharing the winnings. She was too much of a lady to count the money in public and gently pushed the dollars into her purse.

"Now, Rose, we've gotten off to a good start. What do you say we become partners for the day? You pick the horses and I'll place the bets for both of us."

"William, I don't accept charity."

"And, Rose, I don't take the advice of fools. You have an eye for the ponies, that's plain to see."

Brian couldn't believe his ears—"an eye for the ponies"—it was more like William had an eye for Rose. However, it must be said that out of the eight races in the day, Rose picked the winners of six, four of which were long shots. Rose just kept shoving the money into her purse. At the end of the day, Rose had a very heavy purse.

Brian got Rose back to Brooklyn just in time to prepare supper for Mr. Kelley and count her money. Mr. Kelley was busy eating his lamb chop, carrots and mashed potatoes. Rose was busy trying to conceal the fact there was $10,000 in her purse in their bedroom.

"Now, darlin', how was your day?"

"Same as usual, I spent most of it with Mrs. O'Grady."

"You look like you have some color in your cheeks. Did you go to the park?"

"Yes, yes, we went to the park."

"Good, you must do that more often."

Rose washed the dishes and made light conversation the rest of the evening and prayed to God she wouldn't be hearing the thunder of the devil's hooves!

The next morning, Brian called Rose to inform her that William would like her presence at the track that afternoon. Brian was a bit shocked when Rose said she would love to go. Rose was ashamed that she had won $10,000 and did not have a clue who to give it to without Mr. Kelley asking questions. She was certain if she went back to the track she would lose her money. For sure, the Irish saying is true—*Good luck seldom lasts.*

When Brian and Rose arrived at the track, William and his group of men friends were seated exactly in the same spot as the day before. Rose was instructed once again to sit right next to William.

"I'm so pleased you could come, Rose. I'm depending on you to help me pick a winner or two. We'll do the same as yesterday. You pick them Rose, and I'll place the bets for the both of us."

"No, William, I won't accept charity today. I will place me own bets."

"If you insist, so be it."

Rose picked the gray horse for the first race. William needed a bit of convincing to place his bet on a horse that looked like he should be headed back to the barn instead of the winner's circle. But Rose assured him this was the one, or as she put it, "the grace of God is between his saddle and the ground."

It must have been the grace of God because the horse did finish two lengths ahead of the rest but before his saddle came off in the winner's circle, the horse dropped dead.

And so the afternoon went. Rose had more winners than losers, more money than not. William was truly amazed by Rose's talent to pick the winners. He tested her time and time again. Leading her into selecting choices for the daily doubles. The flow of money, thanks to the daily doubles, was exceeding the winnings of yesterday.

At the end of the day, William told Rose, "One of the things that separates professional horseplayers from the rest of the crowd is the ability to stick to their own formula and not pay attention to the post-time odds."

Rose certainly didn't pay attention to the odds, she didn't know where to look for them or truly know what they meant.

"Rose, I'm going to make you a proposition. My newspaper readership is down and you might be the perfect item to give the paper a new spark. I am going to give you your own column. We just have to find a name for it."

"William, I don't know what you're talkin' about. I may be Irish, but me name's not Yates. I'm not a writer. What in the name of God would I be writtin' about?"

"Horses, Rose, horses. You're going to be the new handicapper for New York City's finest newspaper."

"No, no, William, that's against the law. They'll have me arrested."

"Rose, not a bookmaker, a handicapper. You'll be advising the readers on what horses to pick. And, Rose, I won't take no for an answer. We'll call your column, 'The Horseplayers Bible.'"

Brian got Rose back to Brooklyn just in time to prepare supper for Mr. Kelley and count her money. Mr. Kelley was busy eating his pork chop, carrots and mashed potatoes. Rose was busy trying to conceal the fact there was now $20,000 in her purse in the bedroom.

"Now, darlin', what are ya thinkin' about?

You look like you're a million miles away."

Rose was remembering her mother. Whenever Rose did something bad and, worse yet, didn't come forward to say what it was, her mother would rattle off a bit of Irish wisdom.

"You know, Rose, you can't escape telling me what you've done. The devil has all the time in the world. He's just waiting for his day with you."

Rose replied to her husband, "Oh, I was just thinking about Ireland, me mother and the devil."

"The devil? What in God's name is a saint like you thinkin' about the devil for? You're a good woman, Rose. You're the only person I know who's capable of preaching to the devil. But, Rose, it's better to preach to him on a full stomach. Finish your supper and let's go to bed."

The next morning, Rose was sitting at her kitchen table staring at the tea leaves in her cup and looking for a sign. Surely there was a way to get out of this. There was a knock on her door and in walked Brian. Rose was just about to open her mouth when Brian spoke up,

"Surely, Mrs. Kelley, you know the Irish

saying—*Don't tell your troubles to someone who has no pity.* I have no pity for you, no pity. You're probably the richest woman on the block, maybe in the whole neighborhood. And now you are going to be famous, too."

"Oh, Brian, I can't be writtin' a hand-watch-a-ma-call-it column."

"I'll tell you the truth, Mrs. Kelley, William is a very rich and influential man. What he wants, he gets. But I've come to help you. I've arranged for you to spend time with Cadillac Mikey. Cadillac Mikey is our neighborhood bookie. He'll teach you all you need to know about horseracing. You'll write the column for a few months under a pen name, the column will be a big hit, readership will go up and then Cadillac Mikey and I will take over for you. There's no shame in this for you or me. My mother knows it's better to have a son who likes the ponies than a son who drinks."

And so it was. William's newspaper published the first ever column on racing that mentioned God more often than the names of the horses. "The Handicappers Bible" featuring Eve's Picks was an immediate success. Eve's Picks were on more than off and readership did go up.

Of course, Rose's picture never appeared in the paper and Mr. Kelley didn't have the faintest notion that Eve was Rose. Rose arranged to have all of her winnings and salary donated as an anonymous gift to Saint Patrick's school. William did agree to allow Cadillac Mikey and Brian to take over the column. The newspaper skillfully and appropriately killed Eve off. And the column was changed only so slightly...to.... "The Handicappers Bible Featuring Cain and Abel's Selections."

Now surely you must have guessed by now, this story has been a bit of a stretch!

# Rose's Kitchen

Rose Dempsey married Mario Sorrentino in 1981 at the Lady of Angels Catholic Church in Brooklyn. More than 500 people attended their wedding. Rose's mother and father were born in Galway. Mario's father was from a small town near Naples and his mother was raised in Sicily. It came as no surprise to friends and relatives that Mario's family prepared the food for their wedding while Rose's family contributed the liquid refreshment. It's no secret that the Irish aren't known for their cooking ability. Father Cagney, who performed the marriage celebration, gave a good reason for the Irish not being the best of cooks; "There was a time when there was a shortage of food in Ireland, so that accounts for them not knowing what to do with it when they have it."

Rose and Mario were very much in love and continued to have a loving relationship as the years went by. Both families got along and enjoyed spending Sunday's and holidays together. It was a given that Mario's mother, grandmother and aunts would do the cooking. Rose's mother, grandmother and aunts would do the dishes.

Grab yourself a cup of tea or whatever suits you, this story is about food and, in some cases, the lack of it.

The Irish consider food as an irritation that is required to sustain them long enough to win an argument, political debate, or tickles their fancy in the line of conversation. The Italians consider food to be a way of life. Mario's grandfather used to tell him, "Never make love on an empty stomach if you want to please a woman."

Mario didn't understand what one had to do with the other. But as he grew older he did notice that his grandpa was eating all the time and his ever-smiling grandmother was always in her slip even during the winter months.

Mario teased Rose about her cooking. It was never hard for Mario to guess what would be on his plate for dinner. Potatoes every day for sure, mashed, boiled or baked. Cabbage on Mondays, kale on Tuesdays, turnips on Wednesdays, cauliflower on Thursdays, and scallions were intermingled with the vegetable of the day. In the beginning of the marriage, the meat Rose prepared was a mystery to him and very foreign from the meat served in his mother's home. He soon mastered the way to survive eating it. Whether corned beef, mutton, tongue, ham, or sausage, he would sip a glass of red wine, cut a small piece of the meat, and swallow hard.

Fridays, Rose prepared oysters that were quite tasty. Galway, the birthplace of both of Rose's parents, is known as the oyster capital of Ireland. For sure it was in her blood to get it right. And Saturdays, Mario and Rose went out to dinner.

Once a month Rose would bake a loaf of Irish soda bread. Mario would eat a piece and ask Rose to wrap-it-up to take it to work for his employees to enjoy. This pleased Rose. It would have broken her heart to learn Mario gave the loaf to the neighborhood boys who played stickball. The soda bread was hard as a rock and better than any ball imagined. Desserts were not a tradition in Irish families with the exception of fruitcake. Rose's fruitcake did not distinguish itself in the least. Most evenings dessert consisted of custard or

Jell-O.

Mario lived for Sunday's. Mama Sorrentino spent the entire day cooking. There was a table set in the dinning room and another in the kitchen. Cousins, uncles, aunts, sons and daughters would come and go but the food never ran out. The tables were filled with antipasto, minestrone, ravioli, pasta with gravy and home-grown zucchini, eggplant, peppers and tomatoes. All types of chicken dishes: cacciatore, tetrazzini and alla romana. Meat that could be identified by man and prepared with spices and mouthwatering sauces: veal scaloppini, filet mignon Sicilian and Neapolitan pork chops. The bread and desserts were baked by Grandma Sorrentino and heaven sent: cheesecake of many varieties, cannoli, spumoni and torts filled with fresh fruit and cheese.

One Sunday, Mama Sorrentino announced that Mario's Great Uncle Salvatore, who has born and raised in Sicily and now lived in Italy, was coming to Brooklyn to visit his family. Salvatore had never been to America and everyone was very excited. In honor of Salvatore's visit, a flavorful feast of great proportions would be prepared by the women in the family. Rose wanted to be a part of the celebration and told Mario she would prepare a special Irish meal for his great uncle. Mario started to perspire. He could not begin to think of the consequences of Salvatore eating one of Rose's dishes. They might all be killed. After all, it was said Salvatore was the man — The Man. Only two people in Italy got their rings kissed and Salvatore was one of them.

"Oh no, Rose, no need to go to all that trouble. My mother and grandmother will do all the cooking."

"Mario, it won't be any trouble. It just so happens that my cousin Terrance from Dublin will be here the same week as your uncle. Terrance will help me. We'll serve traditional Irish fare that has been handed down for generations."

Mario gave a weak smile and ran off to see Father Cagney.

"Father, there's a crisis in my family. I need your help, the help of the Virgin Mary, Saint Anthony and maybe even Saint Christopher."

Father Cagney listened to Mario and replied, "Mario, do you love your wife?"

"I do, Father, more than life."

"Then let her cook. Your uncle will only

appreciate Italian cooking more than ever before. But I'll tell you what I will do, I will arrange for the Sisters of Mercy to say a rosary the very hour Rose serves her traditional Irish fare!"

And so it was. Cousin Terrance arrived from Dublin. Great Uncle Salvatore arrived from Italy. Mario spent most of the week at church on his knees praying. He searched through his bureau drawers to find every holy medal his mother and grandmother had given him over the years and placed them all around his neck.

It was easy to tell tonight was the night. Mario's body was covered with a rash and his dining room table was covered in fine Irish lace. Mario's father, mother, grandmother, aunts and Great Uncle Salvatore were seated around the table. The hour had arrived. Rose gave the blessing.

Cousin Terrance stood at the kitchen door and began reciting the menu: "The first course from Rose's kitchen this evening will be a prawn cocktail. For those of you not from Ireland, prawns are large shrimp and considered to be a greater delicacy than lobster. The second course from Rose's kitchen will be Irish potato and leek soup served with a bit of sherry. The entrée from Rose's kitchen will be roast pork of loin stuffed with celery and apples served with roasted potatoes and a sauce with garlic grown from Connemara and fresh Galway peas with mushrooms in a sprinkling of Irish brandy. Accompanying the entrée will be brown bread with stone-ground whole-wheat flour from County Tyrone. The evening will end with your choice of desserts from Rose's kitchen, Irish coffee pudding, apple tart and a flan with strawberries from the fields of Killarney. For those of you that would like to partake in something to fill your glass, from Rose's kitchen we have Irish whiskey punch, Black Velvet, which consists of stout and champagne, and Irish coffee made with a special reserve of single malt Irish whisky from County Clare with a dollop of cream from the finest dairy in Donegal. And please, please, do not stir it. For the beautiful lassies, we have tea from all counties of Ireland available in Rose's kitchen."

Mario thought he was dreaming. There was not one morsel of food left on the table and everyone was smiling. Great Uncle Salvatore was kissing Rose's hand. It was the best night of Mario's life and that included his wedding night. He was not disgraced and his family was not disgraced. He could go to Italy and carry his head high. He could go to mass right here in Brooklyn and everyone would greet him with respect.

Mario made a promise that night and one he kept all of his life. Every week he paid the Sisters of Mercy a visit where he diligently carried out all of the chores the sisters had waiting for him.

And in case you are a wee bit curious, it just so happens that Rose's cousin Terrance was the executive chef of one of Dublin's finest restaurants.

# The Biscuit Factory

Albert worked at Dublin's most famous
biscuit factory. He had the important job of
dipping the biscuits into the chocolate. He
was the best chocolate dipper in the factory.
And well he should be. He had been dipping
biscuit's since he was 18. Albert was just about
to turn 35. It was time for Albert to move on.
His cousin Michael in America had arranged
for him to come to New York City. Albert
packed his few possessions and the half-dozen
boxes of chocolate biscuits that he was given
as a going away present and off to the Big
Apple he went.

Cousin Michael had come to America from
Ireland as a child. Most of his family now
lived in Brooklyn. Michael was married to
Katherine and they lived in a large apartment
on Manhattan's east side. Michael and
Katherine allowed Albert to stay in the back
bedroom until he found a good job and could
afford to rent his own apartment in Brooklyn

with the rest of the clan. Each day Michael and Katherine went off to work. Albert would sift through employment sections to search for a job he was suited for. After several weeks of rejection and discouragement Albert was just about ready to give up and go back to Ireland when an opportunity arose. He had made friends with Harry the building elevator man and this particular day Harry told him Mrs. Mellonhouse the Third, who lived in the penthouse apartment, was looking for a professional house painter to paint her living room.

"Well, Harry, what luck for me and Mrs. Mellonhouse. That's what I did for a livin' in Ireland. I was a house painter."

Harry set up the appointment with Rose, Mrs. Mellonhouse's maid who just happened to be Irish. Rose took to Albert like a duck takes to water and an Irishman to a pub. Rose was a widow and had not had a man in her life for over 10 years. Rose reported back to Mrs. Mellonhouse that Albert's painting credentials were impeccable. In fact, in true Irish tradition, Rose embellished slightly by adding that Albert had been commissioned by the president of Ireland to paint both the inside and outside of his residence.

That evening, over dinner, Albert told Michael and Katherine his wonderful news that he had found a job. Michael asked Albert if he needed a few dollars to pay for transportation to and from work. Albert beamed, "No, Cousin Mike, I'm going upstairs and Harry let's me ride free!"

"Upstairs, what do you mean?"

"Mrs. Mellonhouse has hired me."

"How nice, Albert, what will you be doing, a few chores here and there?"

"No, Katherine, I will be painting her living room."

"Albert, I didn't know you had experience as a house painter."

"I don't. I've never held a paint brush in me hand in me life."

"Excuse us for one minute, will you, Albert? Michael, come help me with the dishes. Good God, Michael, Mrs. Mellonhouse owns this building, much of the real estate in Manhattan and the finest department store in the city. You must stop this. You must stop Albert from setting foot in her apartment."

"Don't worry, Katherine, I will handle this."

The next morning Michael had a talk with Albert.

"Albert, you know that Katherine and I are pleased to have you here and we want you to succeed, but, Albert, how can you paint the living room of one of the wealthiest women in Manhattan when you are not qualified to do so?"

"Cousin Mike, I never dipped a biscuit into chocolate either but I became the best biscuit dipper. I've got a lot of confidence in meself, so don't worry, Cousin Mike."

"Albert, I'm not going to worry because I am telling you to call Mrs. Mellonhouse this morning and tell her you are very sorry you will be unable to paint her apartment."

The Irish aren't known for taking advice and certainly not when it comes from another Irishman, so up Albert went to the penthouse suite of Mrs. Mellonhouse the Third. Rose opened the door with her hat and coat on. She was going to spend the morning grocery shopping and running errands. She told Albert the paint and brushes were ready for his masterful touch.

Albert hadn't the foggiest notion how to begin the painting of the room. But he thought surely it couldn't be that difficult. So without delay, he walked over to the paint can and opened it. Très, Très Beaujolais Rouge was the brightest red color he had ever seen in his life. The color made him feel bold and confident. He noticed in the corner of the room there were several white sheets. At first, Albert didn't know what do with them until he finally decided to cut a hole in the center of one and put it over his head. He thought it must have been Rose's idea for him to use the sheets to protect his clothing. There were several brushes on the floor. Albert grabbed the biggest of the lot. His thinking was the bigger the brush the faster it will go. And so it did. Albert's strokes were like the wind near the Irish Sea. Wild and furious did Albert's hand move across the walls of the living room of Mrs. Mellonhouse the Third. He painted with such fury that he failed to notice Très, Très Beaujolais Rouge was not only on the walls but on the antique white chaise, the face of the grandfather clock, the Steinway grand piano, and the Persian rug that covered most of the room. Just as Albert was about to become concerned, Rose opened the door and gave out a scream like a banshee.

"What have ya done, what have ya done!"

"Oh, Rose, please calm yourself and give me a listen. I'll tell you the truth. I'm not a painter."

"Not a painter, then why in God's name did ya say ya were?"

"Me heart was lost to you from the first I saw you coming and going, going and coming. I had to think of some way to get your attention."

"Ya have me attention now, Albert, and you have me pity. You're standing here covered with a sheet that belongs on the floor and Mrs. Mellonhouse's fine rug and furniture is bleeding the bloodiest color red I've ever seen in me life. She'll have you deported back to Ireland to say nothing of the curse that me family will put on you for making me lose me job."

"Rose, you won't lose your job. I'll find a way to make this right."

"Find a way to make it right, will ya? You can't even find a way to get out of the damn sheet. Albert, there are two things that can't be cured—death and stupidity."

Albert was embarrassed. He was in a bit of a pickle. The only good that he could see was the fire in Rose's eyes that made him want to rip the damn sheet off his body, grab Rose, and kiss her lovely Irish lips. And since Albert was not much of a thinker, that's exactly what he did.

Rose hadn't been kissed by a man in over a century. She seized the moment and when it was over, she murmured, "Oh, Albert, you've got a thick skull and now, you've got me heart."

As fate would have it, Rose's brother, Clancy, was a fireman at Station Number 12, only a few blocks from Mrs. Mellonhouse's apartment. Clancy knew how to put out fires and how to paint walls. Clancy was just getting off work when Rose called to replay the tale. He went directly to the apartment to survey the damage. Rose met him at the door.

"Don't be too hard on him, he's the love of me life."

Clancy took one look, made a phone call and before long, four firemen appeared with hose and buckets. When they finished cleaning up, they all grabbed a brush and skillfully stroked the walls with Très, Très Beaujolais Rouge.

Mrs. Mellonhouse the Third was pleased as

punch with the beautifully painted walls of her living room. She wanted to meet the painter. Rose thought long and hard about introducing Albert to Mrs. Mellonhouse, but then she had to admit even wise men have faults. However, Rose did tell her employer that Albert really wasn't a painter, he was a biscuit maker. Well, not quite, he was a biscuit chocolate dipper.

But as fate would have it, Rose was quite the baker and soon Rose and Albert's chocolate biscuits placed in a Très, Très Beaujolais Rouge box was the most sought after gourmet item in the finest department store in Manhattan.

# The Beat Of Two Drums

Rose McGuire was 13 years old and a student at Saint Patrick's Catholic school in Brooklyn. Since her kindergarten days she was one of the students selected to perform in the auditorium on Saint Patrick's Day. Rose had been taking Irish step-dancing classes since she was three years old. She had always loved the classes and the dancing but now felt embarrassed and thought it was not in keeping with the modern world of the 1990s.

Never one to shy away from stating her opinion, Rose told Sister Regina that Irish step-dancing was not "in vogue" anymore in Brooklyn and she did not want to step-dance this Saint Patrick's Day, which was coming up in three weeks.

Sister Regina replied as only an Irish, elderly, saintly nun would, "Rose, in the name of the Father, Son, and Holy Ghost, you will be step-dancin' along with the other girls on Saint Patrick's Day."

Never one to give up when she wanted her way, Rose confided in her best friend, Mary Frances, that she was not going to be step-dancing on that stage on Saint Patrick's Day. Mary Frances was one of four girls that were going to be step-dancing along with Rose. Mary Frances began to get a little worried. She knew Rose could be crafty and often got into a bit of trouble and sometimes she got into that trouble, too.

Rose listened to and danced to the popular music of the 1990s, songs by Michael Bolton, the New Kids on the Block, and her very favorite group the Spice Girls. Rose was fairly sure the girls selected to dance did not want to be step-dancing either.

Rose invited the girls to her house after Mass on Sunday. She told her mother the girls would be coming over to practice their step-dancing. "Mum, we want to be sure each step is perfect so we won't disappoint Sister Regina and the audience."

Mary Francis, Deidre, Colleen and Molly were seated comfortably in the parlor of Rose's home happily munching away on Irish ginger snap cookies prepared by Rose's grandmother, Philomena.

Rose knew she had to be very convincing in her quest to have all of the girls agree not to step-dance on the stage on St. Patrick's Day. "I asked you to come to my home to address an important matter. Are we Irish or are we Americans?"

At first there was silence in the parlor. Then Molly spoke up, "What a foolish question, Rose, you know we are all Irish."

Almost in sync, the rest of the girls blurred out, "We're all Irish!"

Colleen added, "If we weren't, we wouldn't be step-dancing on the stage on Saint Patrick's Day."

Rose's face turned very red and then she screamed at the top of her lungs, "We're not Irish; we're Americans, born here in Brooklyn." The words were not out of Rose's mouth very long when Philomena entered the parlor.

"Rose, I was in the kitchen fixin' another batch of Irish Ginger Snaps for you and the girls but I don't think you will be needin' them. Maybe the Irish girls down the block would enjoy them!"

Rose knew she was in hot water now. Rose dearly loved her grandmother and she didn't want to hurt her feelings or disrespect her. She also knew the Irish expression *No flies on her* applied to her grandmother. Grandmother Philomena was well-read and well-informed. The only choice Rose had at this moment was to try and talk her way out of the situation.

"Grandmother, Irish step-dancing is old-fashioned and very Irish. I'm an American. I've never even been to Ireland."

Philomena took a deep breath and what came to mind was the Irish saying—*It's difficult to put an old head on a young shoulder.* "Rose, it's true you were born in Brooklyn, which is in America. Meself and your ancestors were born on a tiny beautiful green island that dates back to 600 years BC. That's before the man you read about in your catechism was born."

"Who is that, grandmother?"

"It's himself, Jesus Christ. Irish soil is in the souls of your ancestors and in the pores of your skin."

Rose thought Grandmother Philomena was always a bit dramatic in her storytelling but that's what made her so interesting and convincing.

Philomena went on to tell Rose all about

the history of Ireland since the Celtic tribes arrived and the travails that led to the Easter Rebellion, acting out a bit of it herself. Mary Francis, Deidre, Colleen and Molly were still in the parlor and utterly mesmerized.

"Rose, if you have already studied American history, you know that eight of the men who signed the Declaration of Independence were of Irish descent. It was the long perfectly formed fingers of an Irishman, with such beautiful handwriting that helped to carefully script each word of that document. Rose, many great Americans have Irish blood running through their veins. American presidents, at least 17 of them were of Irish heritage.

"Rose, I know you want to visit Texas one day, well, Sam Houston, the first president of Texas, his ancestors came from Ireland." Rose's eyes truly lit up at the mention of Texas. Grandmother Philomena, such a wise woman, carefully elected to slip in a word about Texas, and even though it pained her so, she omitted mentioning Ireland's literary tradition and the Irish American writers, F. Scott Fitzgerald and Eugene O'Neill.

"Rose, do you know much about the step-dancin'?"

"Grandmother, I know the steps, believe me I know the steps."

"Rose, it's the history of the dance you should know. It was established to preserve and strengthen the Irish culture. The dance goes back to the late 1800s. And believe it or not, Rose, even though we're in the 1990s, there is a group that performs all over the world with their step-dancin' and I think I read they're going to be at Radio City Music Hall before the year is done."

"Grandmother, Radio City Music Hall, I'd give anything to perform there."

"Well, you had better start practicing your step-dancin'! Just for me own sake, Rose, what was your plan for Saint Patrick's Day, were you not going to get on the stage?"

"Oh no, grandmother, the girls and I would have been on the stage performing a new dance and singing as well."

"And what Irish tune was that going to be?"

"Grandmother, if the girls are willing, we can perform it for you now."

"Oh, Rose, I'd be delighted to hear it. Let me get a cup of tea and I'll be right back."

Just for fun, over the past several months,

Rose taught Mary Frances, Deidre, Colleen and Molly the lyrics and the moves to one of her very favorite songs. The girls always followed Rose's direction because when they were with Rose they had a good time. Following Rose's lead, the five girls stood in front of Grandmother Philomena and began singing and dancing.

Grandmother Philomena simply sipped her tea through the entire performance, spilled not a drop and never changed the expression on her face.

When the girls were through, she spoke, "Well, you know, Rose, there are five of them and there are five of you. And, as you know, Rose, all five of them are British and all five of you are Irish. You certainly have the Latin rhythms and the salsa and samba steps down pat. My only critique is, when you're movin' to the right you might consider shaken those hips a bit more."

There was silence in the parlor for quite some time. At last, Grandmother Philomena spoke, "It's such a damn shame Sister Regina will be missing such a fine performance," then she began to laugh and Rose, Mary Francis, Deidre, Colleen and Molly followed suit.

There is an Irish saying—*Say but little and say it well.*

"My darlin' granddaughter Rose, you indeed have that American spirit and you indeed have that Irish wit. You have the best of both worlds' you are an Irish American."

# A Proper Name

Dennis and Claire Hogan were sitting in the waiting room of Dr. Patel's office for what would be their last visit before the birth of their first child. They had just returned from a tour of the new maternity section of the hospital where their child would be born. Claire was impressed with the modern equipment and technologies available for a smooth delivery. After a bit of a wait, the nurse ushered them into the doctor's office.

Dr. Patel was a young doctor who received his training from one of the leading medical schools in the United States. "Good morning, how are the both of you today?"

Always one to be honest, Dennis replied, "I'm a little nervous and can't sleep much. And, oh, by the way, doctor, I hope you don't mind my grandmother wanted to meet you so she will be joining us shortly." With that, Dr. Patel's nurse opened the door and in walked Rose Rafferty.

"It's my pleasure to meet you, Mrs.

Rafferty. I have enjoyed these nine months getting to know your grandson and his wife."

"Oh, to be sure they're a wonderful pair."

"I was just about to ask Claire how she was feeling today."

"Doctor, I'm calm and cool as a cucumber."

Dennis smiled and said, "It must be all that time you spend standing on your head."

"Yes, the yoga helps calm me."

Rose piped in, "So be it if that's your cup of tea. I'd be as dizzy as a drunken sailor."

Dr. Patel took Claire into his examining room and when they returned to his office he told Dennis and Rose that the birth would be within the next 48 hours. Dennis' grandmother asked if she could have a bit of a word with the doctor in private. Dennis and Claire understood quite well Irish grandmothers so it really didn't surprise them and thank goodness the doctor nodded and Dennis and Claire left the room.

"Doctor, I am a grandmother many times, seven times to be exact, and they're all grandsons. Before I die, I would like a granddaughter. I have saved up a considerable sum of money which I am prepared to offer you if you will deliver me a granddaughter."

The doctor was not exactly stunned but he was not sure how to respond. He took a deep breath and in his most professional manner he replied, "Mrs. Rafferty, we are in the 21st century and medical science has progressed at almost the speed of light, however, I don't have the capability to accommodate you. Thanks to modern medicine we can determine what the sex of the child is early on, but I, nor any other doctor, cannot magically deliver the desired gender of the child to please a parent, or, as in your case, a grandmother. It is because of modern medicine that I do know the sex of the child, Dennis and Claire have decided not to be told what the sex is, they want to be surprised."

A wide grin came across Roses face. "So after all those fancy words, you're a bit of a devil and that's okay with me, the money's yours, just whisper in me ear, is it a boy or is it a girl."

"Oh, Mrs. Rafferty, I can't be bribed, you know doctors take an oath."

Always one to have the last word, Rose replied, "and so do elected officials!"

Going home in the car, Dennis asked his grandmother about the nature of the conversation she had with the doctor.

"Oh, he was getting me up to speed on all this modern technology and how babies are delivered."

Claire joining the conversation saying, "it sure has changed since you gave birth to Dennis' father."

"It certainly has. They just kept coming with the boiling water and with all of me howling, our chickens were too frightened to lay their eggs." It was not a moment too soon that the car pulled up in front of Rose's home.

That night, Dennis and Claire had a simple dinner and a serious conversation. Whether their child was a boy or a girl, they had not selected a name for the child. Dennis was named after his father and his two brothers were John and Patrick and their sons had very Irish names, Brandon, Colin, Keegan, Kyle, Liam, Ryan and Shane. Claire truly did not want to pick an Irish name for a boy or for a girl. Dennis more or less agreed with Claire, he thought the child should have a name that is unique and that is not associated with their nationally. They stayed up half the night writing lists of names and finally decided on Madison if it is a girl and Wyatt if it is a boy.

The next morning, Dennis and Claire called their parents and told them the arrival of a new family member would be soon. They told their parents the names they had selected and both sets of parents thought the names were right in keeping for today's world. Even Claire's mother, Margaret, thought the names were a good choice. However, Dennis' father said one person in their family might not agree!

Yesterday was uneventful and all of the family members were hoping today would be the day that Claire would deliver. Dennis' brother John had just received notice that he would be representing his firm in a meeting to be held in Germany in three days. The one thing that all members of their Irish Catholic family agreed upon was the child's baptism should be as soon as possible. In this case, John was going to be the godfather so they must arrange for the baptism to be done before he leaves.

The clock had not yet struck noon when Claire very calmly called Dennis to the kitchen and said, "Start boiling the water!"

Dennis drove Claire to the hospital, called his grandmother, parents and siblings and went into the labor room to be with Claire. Claire always said she loved being married to an Irishman because of their great wit. Dennis was hoping she'd find him funny under her current set of circumstances.

Dennis and Claire's entire family clan were sitting in the maternity waiting room. The talk of the group was the fact there was no doubt this new child was going to be a boy. That's the way it was in this family, including on Claire's side. Claire was the only girl in her family. Dr. Patel stopped in the waiting room to say hello to the family members before he went on to the delivery room.

Rose greeted him with, "Doctor, I was thinkin' we should all make a wager as to whether the child's going to be a boy or are girl. Would you like to participate?"

"No thank you, Mrs. Rafferty." Dr. Patel walked down the hall to the delivery room with quicker steps than usual.

What seemed like a lifetime were only a few hours. Dennis came bouncing down the hall to make the announcement that he was the proud father of… a daughter. The family members were elated and Rose looking smug as a bug in a rug, could not have been happier than if her late husband were to be resurrected from his grave of 20 years.

Dennis told everyone that Claire was fine and the baby was fine and they both would be able to come home in two days. Dennis relayed to the family that he and Claire decided to name their daughter, Madison. All cheered except for one.

"Madison, like in the avenue?"

"Yes, grandmother, like in the avenue."

"Is that even a proper name?"

"Grandmother, it's a modern-day name. Now, let's go home and celebrate and I'll call Father Cassidy to see if he can come to the hospital tomorrow to baptize our darling little girl."

The very next day, Dennis, Claire, their baby daughter along with all family members and Dr. Patel, who was pleased that he had been invited, were seated in the hospital chapel. Father Cassidy told John Hogan, the godfather, and his wife Eileen, the godmother, to step forward and asked them, "Who presents this child to receive the Sacrament of Baptism."

They replied, "We do."

After reciting the Holy Baptism liturgy, Father Cassidy began to pour the water on the head of Dennis and Claire's baby daughter, while saying, "Rose Margaret Hogan, I baptize you in the Name of the Father and of the Son and of the Holy Spirit. Amen."

Dr. Patel, now, practically a member of the Hogan family, asked Dennis and Claire why they decided not to name their daughter Madison. Claire told him she remembered an old Irish saying—*If you ate honey while you were pregnant, your baby will have a sweet disposition. If you ate spicy foods, you would have trouble on your hands!* "Well, I love spicy foods and ate them the entire time I was pregnant. And what's more, life is so much more interesting when you have a little spice in your life. Dennis and I agreed that Grandmother Rose makes our lives very interesting and Rose is a proper name for an Irish girl."